CLIMATE CHANGE

JADE ZORA SCIBILIA

PowerKiDS press

NEW YORK

Published in 2019 by The Rosen Publishing Group, Inc.
29 East 21st Street, New York, NY 10010

Editor: Hannah Fields
Cover Design: Michael Flynn
Interior Layout: Tanya Dellaccio

Photo Credits: Cover (background) Cammie Czuchnicki/Shutterstock.com; cover Paul Souders/Corbis Documentary/ Getty Images; p. 5 Marzolino/Shutterstock.com; p. 6 Julien Hautcoeur/Shutterstock.com; p. 7 gagarych/ Shutterstock.com; p. 9 Handout/Getty Images News/Getty Images; p. 10 Bildagentur Zoonar GmbH/Shutterstock.com; p. 11 Henri Vandelanotte/Shutterstock.com; p. 13 Vitoriano Junior/Shutterstock.com; p. 15 Shchipkova Elena/ Shutterstock.com; p. 16 https://commons.wikimedia.org/wiki/File:COP21_participants_-_30_Nov_2015_ (23430273715).jpg; p. 17 Drop of Light/Shutterstock.com; p. 19 SkyLynx/Shutterstock.com; p. 20 Rawpixel.com/ Shutterstock.com; p. 21 Syda Productions/Shutterstock.com.

Cataloging-in-Publication Data

Names: Scibilia, Jade Zora.
Title: Climate change / Jade Zora Scibilia.
Description: New York : PowerKids Press, 2019. | Series: Spotlight on weather and natural disasters | Includes glossary and index.
Identifiers: LCCN ISBN 9781508168836 (pbk.) | ISBN 9781508168812 (library bound) | ISBN 9781508168843 (6 pack)
Subjects: LCSH: Climatic changes--Juvenile literature. | Climatic changes--Effect of human beings on--Juvenile literature. | Climatic changes--Government policy--Juvenile literature. | Global warming--Juvenile literature.
Classification: LCC QC903.15 S35 2019 | DDC 363.738'74--dc23

Manufactured in the United States of America

CPSIA Compliance Information: Batch #CS18PK For further information contact Rosen Publishing, New York, New York at 1-800-237-9932.

CONTENTS

CHAPTER ONE

WHAT IS GLOBAL CLIMATE CHANGE?

Have you ever heard people talk about global climate change? This means the long-term change in Earth's climate that's partly caused by human activity.

When you think of climate, you might first think about the weather. However, climate and weather aren't the same thing. Weather is the state of the atmosphere in a particular place over a short period of time. Climate is the big-picture view of what happens in the **environment** of a whole region over a much longer period of time. It takes into account patterns such as average temperature, rainfall, and sunlight.

Weather can be rainy, snowy, cloudy, or sunny. It often varies from day to day. In contrast, climates include conditions that remain mostly the same. Climates can be hot and **arid**, like in a desert; they can be **humid** and warm, like in a jungle; or they can be very cold, like in the Arctic region.

There are many kinds of environments around the world. One **continent** can have deserts, forests, plains, and more.

CHAPTER TWO

A WARMING PLANET

Climate scientists are worried about broad, rapid changes in our global climate. They're concerned about the warming of our planet as a whole.

It might seem silly to look at the average temperature of the entire planet, especially when you compare the freezing temperatures at the North and South Poles to the **sweltering** temperatures along the equator. But scientists can learn a lot by looking at the average surface temperatures across the planet. These

Desert landscapes have very little vegetation because of their hot and arid climates.

Because the global temperature continues to rise, snow and ice in the Arctic region are at risk of melting.

averages can reveal patterns of **positive** or **negative** changes across large regions.

For example, the average global temperature in 2016 was 1.69°Fahrenheit (0.94°C) warmer than the planet's average temperature for the entire 20th century! While this might not sound like much of a change, it actually has a huge effect on the global climate.

CHAPTER THREE

WHAT HAPPENS WHEN EARTH WARMS?

When average global surface temperatures increase, even by a few degrees, we witness changes to all different kinds of climates, which affect everyone and everything on the planet.

As the planet warms, polar ice melts, sea levels rise, animal and plant ranges shift, and **extreme** weather events (such as hurricanes and droughts) become more frequent and more severe.

One of the main problems with global climate change is that it's happening more quickly. Each year, the effects of climate change compound each other. This means that a change in one issue causes an increased change in another issue. For example, when polar ice melts, global sea levels rise; when sea levels rise, there's more surface water warming the planet, so even more polar ice melts. These changes are steps in a never-ending cycle.

Summertime Arctic sea ice has decreased by at least 12 percent every 10 years since the 1970s. Compare the differences in summertime ice coverage from 2001 to 2007. It's possible that, at some point during this century, we'll witness a summer when there is no Arctic sea ice at all.

AUGUST 2001

AUGUST 2007

Melt Ponds

Water

Open Water

CHAPTER FOUR

CLIMATE CHANGE AND CARBON DIOXIDE

Climate scientists agree that climate change is directly linked to human activity, including **industrialization**, manufacturing, and the burning of **fossil fuels**.

Manufacturing often makes heavy demands on the environment. It requires the importation and transportation of raw materials and people from the

By examining air bubbles trapped deep in the polar ice caps, scientists can figure out how much carbon dioxide was in the air thousands of years ago. They can compare it to how much is in the air now. Studies show that the amount of carbon dioxide in our atmosphere has increased, especially within the last 10 years.

surrounding areas—or from across the globe. Then, finished products are shipped to markets around the world.

This is often accomplished with energy created by burning fossil fuels. Unfortunately, this releases carbon dioxide into our atmosphere. Carbon dioxide is a greenhouse gas. Greenhouse gases are gases that trap heat in the atmosphere surrounding our planet instead of letting the heat escape to outer space.

CHAPTER FIVE

THE GREENHOUSE EFFECT

Carbon dioxide is the most common greenhouse gas, but there are others, including methane. These gases are a problem because of the greenhouse effect.

The greenhouse effect can be a good thing. It's what keeps Earth's climate stable and capable of supporting life. Sunlight passes through the atmosphere like it's the roof of a greenhouse and warms Earth's surface during the day. At night, Earth cools and releases heat.

Unfortunately, when the atmosphere includes too much carbon dioxide (and other greenhouse gases), heat cannot escape to space. It bounces back down to the surface, and the planet gets warmer and warmer. This is what causes global climate change.

Greenhouse gases in Earth's atmosphere work like the roof of a greenhouse. Heat and light from the sun come in, and then carbon dioxide and other greenhouse gases trap the heat inside, keeping Earth warm. If too much heat becomes trapped, then the planet can't cool down.

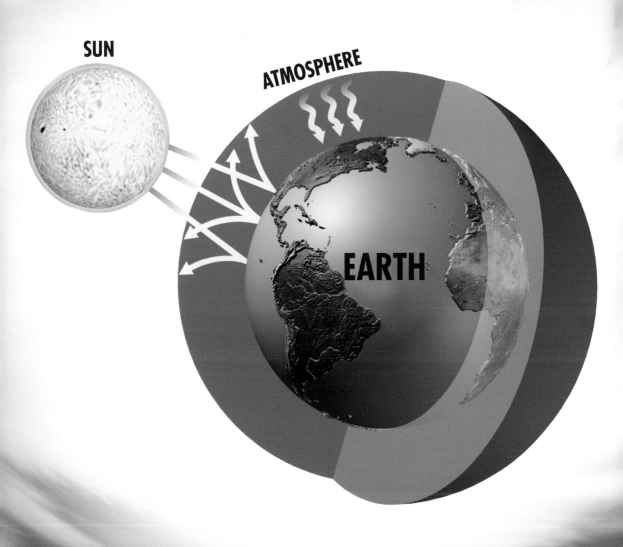

SUN

ATMOSPHERE

EARTH

CHAPTER SIX

WILDLIFE ON A WARMER PLANET

Global warming affects plants and animals, too. Their ranges shift from one place to another in response to changes in climate. A range is a region where certain animal populations live or particular types of plants grow.

Rising temperatures affect climates across the planet differently. For example, polar regions are shrinking because of the rapid melting of sea ice. Animals that live in these areas, such as polar bears, are losing their **habitats**. In the **savanna**, warmer temperatures mean that water sources are drying up and plants are struggling to grow. This affects large animals, such as African elephants, which need to consume hundreds of pounds of plants each day to survive.

Polar bears are famously affected by global climate change. They need sea ice for places to have babies and to rest when they hunt for seals, which are their main source of food. As polar ice melts and sea levels rise, polar bears could become **extinct**.

CHAPTER SEVEN

GLOBAL SOLUTIONS TO A GLOBAL PROBLEM

Climate change is a global problem requiring a global **solution**. Every climate, country, and person is affected by changes to our planet's atmosphere.

Major climate changes can cause serious problems that hurt people. They can also cause conflicts between nations. For example, when sea levels rise, coastal areas—even whole cities or islands—can be flooded by

At the 2015 UN Climate Change Conference, representatives adopted the Paris Agreement. This agreement set standards to try to limit the rise of the global temperature by reducing greenhouse gases. As of January 2018, 195 countries have signed the agreement.

UNITED NATIONS GENERAL ASSEMBLY

the ocean. This can shift the borders of countries and force people to move away from the water, which can cause conflict.

The United Nations (UN) is an **international** organization of governments. It tries to further **cooperation** between all countries. The UN holds annual meetings called UN Climate Change Conferences. During these conferences, representatives from all over the world meet to talk about concerns about climate change, answers for the problem, and ways to reduce the greenhouse gases we create.

CHAPTER EIGHT

ALTERNATIVE AND RENEWABLE ENERGY

Instead of burning fossil fuels to create energy, we can use renewable energy sources. Fossil fuels are the result of plant and animal matter that has been breaking down for millions of years. These fuels are limited; once we take them from the environment, they're gone. Renewable energy sources, however, renew themselves over time.

There are many sources of energy on our planet—the sun, the wind, and even the ocean. Solar power is energy harnessed from sunlight using solar panels. Wind power is energy that comes from shifting air masses. It can be harnessed with wind **turbines**. Tidal power is energy that comes from the ocean's tides. It can be harnessed with tidal turbines. All of these are renewable, clean, and safe energy sources.

Wind turbines are just one way we can harness a renewable energy source.

CHAPTER NINE

WHAT CAN YOU DO?

To limit global warming, the biggest polluters, such as large manufacturing companies and many large farms, must make the biggest changes. But there are small steps that each of us can take, too.

Encourage your political representatives to keep climate change in mind when they pass legislation, or laws. Reduce, reuse, and recycle to limit the amount of waste you produce. If you must travel or commute, use buses or trains. You could also carpool, which means

Together, we can change the world. By taking small actions like recycling, commuting less, and planting more trees, we can improve the air quality of our local environment.

to share a ride with a group of people. Better yet, ride your bike or walk! Celebrate important events, such as birthdays, by planting trees. Plants are amazing because they absorb carbon dioxide from the air—and they create oxygen, which we need to breathe.

Making these small changes to your life will reduce the amount of pollution and greenhouse gases in Earth's atmosphere.

CHAPTER TEN

SCIENCE TO THE RESCUE!

It can be scary to think about the effects of global climate change and a warming planet: extreme weather events, animals and people in danger, sea levels on the rise, and habitats in trouble. It's because of these dangers that we need to take climate change seriously, listen to climate scientists' warnings, and take action as a community and as individuals.

With every challenge comes many opportunities. You can make a real difference by changing your lifestyle to become less wasteful. You can encourage leaders to make changes in businesses that pollute our atmosphere. And you can study science, engineering, and mathematics. Who knows? You could be the next scientist who discovers new ways to improve our energy use, save animals from extinction, or remove greenhouse gases from the atmosphere!

22

GLOSSARY

arid (AA-ruhd) Receiving little or no rain.

continent (KAHN-tuh-nuhnt) One of the seven great masses of land on Earth.

cooperation (koh-ah-puh-RAY-shuhn) The act of working with others to get something done.

environment (en-VY-ruhn-muhnt) The conditions that surround a living thing and affect the way it lives.

extinct (ihk-STINKT) No longer existing.

extreme (ihk-STREEM) Very great in degree.

fossil fuel (FAH-suhl FYOOL) A fuel—such as coal, oil, or natural gas—that is formed in the earth from dead plants or animals.

habitat (HAA-buh-tat) The natural home for plants, animals, and other living things.

humid (HYOO-mihd) To have a lot of moisture in the air.

industrialization (ihn-duh-stree-uh-luh-ZAY-shuhn) The process of building and operating factories in an area.

international (ihn-tuhr-NAA-shuh-nuhl) Made up of people or groups from different countries.

negative (NEH-guh-tiv) In a bad way.

positive (PAH-suh-tiv) In a good way.

savanna (suh-VAA-nuh) A grassland with scattered patches of trees.

sweltering (SWEL-tuh-ring) Very hot.

solution (suh-LOO-shuhn) A way to solve a problem.

turbine (TUHR-byn) An engine with blades that are caused to spin by pressure from water, steam, or air.

INDEX

PRIMARY SOURCE LIST

Page 5
Climate map. Document. Created by Paul Vidal de La Blache in *Atlas Classique*. 1894. From Shutterstock.com.

Page 9
Satellite images showing polar sea ice. From U.S. satellites. Created in August 2001 and 2007. Courtesy of the U.S. Geological Survey.

Page 16
Heads of delegations at the 2015 UN Climate Change Conference. Photograph. November 29, 2015. Paris, France.

WEBSITES